Merry Christmas,
Everywhere!

Merry Christmas, EVERYWHERE!

By Arlene Erlbach With Herb Erlbach

Illustrated by Sharon Lane Holm

THE MILLBROOK PRESS ⭐ BROOKFIELD, CONNECTICUT

To Tony and Antoinette Copeland, true Christmas celebrants,

and Matt Erlbach, who sings beautiful Christmas carols. —AE

To Chuck Becker, who embraces the true spirit of Christmas everyday. — HE

For Nathan—welcome, little one! —SLH

Library of Congress Cataloging-in-Publication Data
Erlbach, Arlene.
Merry Christmas, everywhere! / by Arlene Erlbach with Herb Erlbach;
illustrated by Sharon Lane Holm.
p. cm.
Includes bibliographical references
Summary: Presents Christmas greetings and traditions, with related
activities, from around the world.
ISBN 0-7613-1956-5 (lib. bdg.)   ISBN 0-7613-1699-X (pbk.)
1. Christmas—Juvenile literature. [1. Christmas. 2. Christmas decorations.
3. Christmas cookery. 4. Handicraft.] I. Erlbach, Herb. II. Holm, Sharon
Lane, ill. III. Title.
GT4985.5 .E77 2002   394.2663—dc21   2001044758

Published by The Millbrook Press, Inc.
2 Old New Milford Road
Brookfield, Connecticut 06804
www.millbrookpress.com

Contents

Acknowledgments

This book would not have been possible without help from all these wonderful people and organizations.

Adotey Addo

Angie Anagnostopoulos

The Akintunde Family

Karen Arnold

The Australian Consulate

Richard Backwell

Elsa Berrios

The Consulate of Bolivia

Fadi Boulos

British Consulate General

Canadian Consulate General

Virginia Castillo

Rosa Cruz

The Embassy of Ethiopia

Carmen Folkes

The Consulate of France

Consulate General of Ghana

The Embassy of Ghana

Icelandic Consulate General of Chicago

Consulate General of India

Invest in France Agency

Consulate General of Greece Office for
    Educational Affairs

The Jamaican Consulate

The Embassy of Japan

Carlos Menendez

Milo Ostojic

Janet T. Peterson, World Book Publishing

Edna Rivera

Robertson's Candy

Irena Sidorski

Luz Trevino

Consulate General of Venezuela

Dr. Robert and Elizabeth Winter

Introduction

To Christians all over the world, December 25 is an important day of the year. It's Christmas, the anniversary of Jesus Christ's birth. Christmas is observed by more than a billion people in more than one hundred countries around the world.

Nobody is sure of the exact date of Christ's birth. December 25 was chosen for a good reason. Long ago, people held festivals in late December hoping that winter would end. They built bonfires, had feasts, and exchanged gifts. Since people already celebrated at this time of year, church officials thought this would be a good time to observe Christ's birth.

Not everyone celebrates Christmas the same way. Some people observe Christmas on a date other than December 25. In some countries, people honor Christmas-related holidays such as Saint Nicholas Day or Saint Lucia Day, too.

In certain parts of the world, festivities last through January 6 or even longer. January 6 is the Epiphany, or Three Kings' Day. This is when the Three Kings brought gifts to Jesus, and the date some people exchange gifts. The period from December 25 through January 6 is the twelve days of Christmas.

In this book, you'll discover many Christmas traditions. You'll read about activities you can add to your own celebration. You can share these customs with your family and friends to honor the most widely celebrated holiday in the world.

Australia

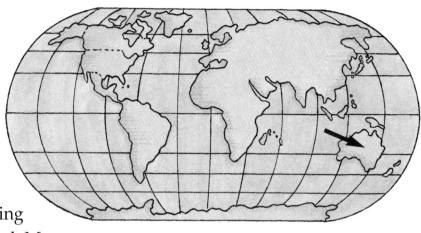

Greeting: *Happy Christmas* or *Merry Christmas*
The official language of Australia is English.

In Australia, Santa might not visit in a red fur-trimmed outfit. Sometimes he arrives on water skis and wears a red bathing suit. Christmas occurs during summer in Australia, when children are out of school. Many Australians eat their Christmas dinner at a picnic on the beach or at a barbecue in their yard.

Because the weather in Australia is so warm at Christmas, some children leave out a glass of cold lemonade for Santa. They might serve cakes called lamingtons, too. You can make lamingtons for Santa and your family and friends. Here's how:

What you'll need:

- one 9-ounce box of yellow cake mix
- one 8- by 8-inch (20- by 20-cm) square cake pan
- chocolate frosting
- a knife to spread the frosting
- dried coconut

What to do:

1. Bake the cake according to package instructions.

2. Let the cake cool.

3. Cut the cake into squares.

4. Frost the top and sides of the cake squares with frosting.

5. Cover the top and the sides of the frosted cake squares with coconut.

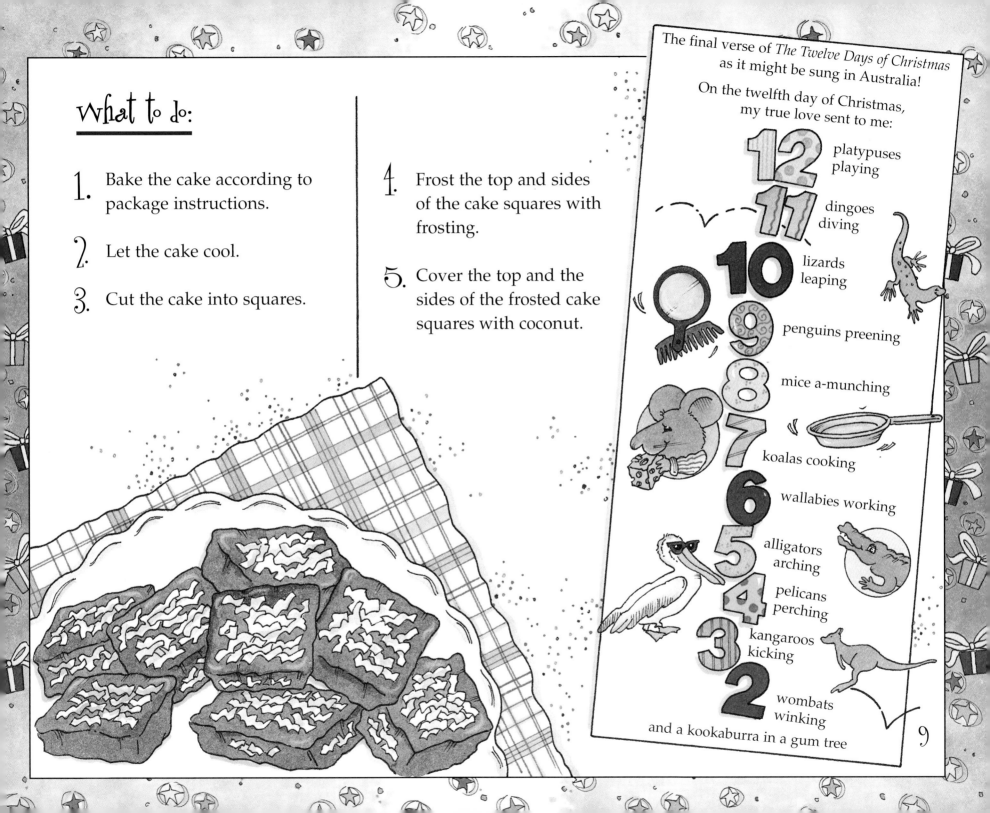

The final verse of *The Twelve Days of Christmas* as it might be sung in Australia!

On the twelfth day of Christmas, my true love sent to me:

12 platypuses playing

11 dingoes diving

10 lizards leaping

9 penguins preening

8 mice a-munching

7 koalas cooking

6 wallabies working

5 alligators arching

4 pelicans perching

3 kangaroos kicking

2 wombats winking

and a kookaburra in a gum tree

Bolivia

Greeting: *Feliz Navidad,* pronounced *feh-LEES nah-VEE-dad,* which means "Happy Nativity." The greeting is in Spanish.

In Bolivia, some people bring roosters to midnight mass on Christmas Eve. This symbolizes the legend about a rooster that was the first animal to announce the birth of Jesus. Bolivians call this service *Misa del Gallo,* which means "Mass of the Rooster."

Bolivian children leave their shoes or stockings out hoping for presents from *El Niño Jesus,* which means "Baby Jesus" in Spanish. He knows exactly what they want. The children place clay models of what they'd like for Christmas by the figure of Jesus in their family's nativity scene.

Make models of what you'd like for Christmas and display them. Maybe that's what you'll receive.

What you'll need:

- air-drying clay
- poster paint
- paintbrushes

10

What to do:

1. Shape your clay into what you would like for Christmas.

2. When your clay dries, decorate with poster paint.

3. Put your items by the manger in your family's nativity scene, or display them under your Christmas tree.

If some of your wishes are too difficult to make from clay, draw pictures of them. Or you can cut them from catalogs or magazines and then glue them to small squares of paper.

Canada

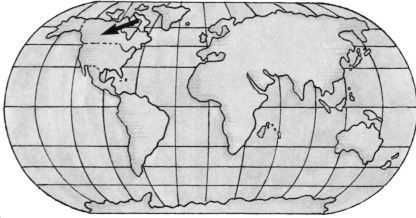

Greeting: *Merry Christmas*, unless you live in the province of Quebec, where French is the official language. Then your greeting would be *Joyeux Noël*, pronounced *joy-yooh no-el*, which means "Joyous Christmas."

If you lived in eastern Canada, you'd receive a barley toy or a chicken bone in your Christmas stocking. Barley toys aren't toys. Chicken bones aren't bones. Both are candies sold in eastern Canada during the Christmas season. A chicken bone is a cinnamon-flavored hard candy filled with chocolate. A barley toy is a red or yellow hard candy on a stick. The candy is shaped like a toy or Santa Claus. Barley toys usually weigh about an ounce (28 grams). But some barley toys look like train engines and weigh 2½ pounds (1 kilogram).

    You can make a treat similar to barley toys for your family and friends. Here's how:

What you'll need:

- a saucepan
- one cup of water
- 6-ounce box of red or yellow gelatin dessert mix
- a wooden spoon
- 8-inch (20-cm) square pan
- cookie cutters
- craft sticks

red fruit **jell** gelatin dessert

NET WT 6 OZ.

12

What to do:

1. With adult help, boil the water. Remove from the stove and put the gelatin into the water. Stir well until all the gelatin crystals disappear.

2. Pour the gelatin mixture into the pan.

3. Place the pan with the gelatin mixture into the refrigerator for about three hours.

4. When the gelatin mixture is set, use the cookie cutters to cut out shapes from the gelatin.

5. Insert a craft stick into each shape.

Your barley toys won't be hard, like the ones in Canada. They'll be slightly wiggly instead, but they'll still be fun to eat and share.

13

Ethiopia

Greeting: *Melkm Ganna*, pronounced *MEL-calm GEH-nuh*, which means "Wishing You a Happy Christmas. The greeting is in Amharic.

Ethiopian children don't celebrate on December 25. They observe Christmas on January 7, instead. That's Christ's birthdate according to the Ethiopian calendar. On January 19, Ethiopians observe Timkat, Christ's baptism. Timkat lasts for three days. On the first day of Timkat, priests collect church scrolls containing the Ten Commandments. They carry them to tents where people come to pray. The scrolls are so sacred that priests protect them with umbrellas decorated with gold embroidery.

Make an umbrella for Timkat. Hang it in your home from January 7 through January 21, the days of the Ethiopian Christmas season.

What you'll need:

- one sheet of construction paper, 8½ by 11 inches (22 by 28 cm)
- a pencil
- scissors
- gold glitter pen or gold crayon
- strip of gold paper measuring 2 by 11 inches (5 by 28 cm)
- glue
- two 4-inch (10-cm) craft sticks
- 4-inch (10-cm) scrap of leftover gold paper to cover the point and handle of the umbrella.

14

What to do:

1. Fold the sheet of paper in half.

2. Draw an outline of half of an umbrella.

3. Cut around your outline. Make sure not to cut on the fold.

4. Unfold your umbrella.

5. Use the gold crayon or glitter pen to draw gold embroidery on the umbrella.

6. Glue the 11-inch (28-cm) strip of gold paper to the bottom of the umbrella. Cut to make fringe.

7. Add the craft sticks to make a handle and a point on top.

8. Decorate the point and handle with gold paper, the glitter pen, or crayon.

On Christmas, Ethiopians eat dinner from a shared plate. Each person scoops up a serving with a piece of pancake-like bread, called *injera*. The *injera* is like a fork, spoon, and plate.

15

France

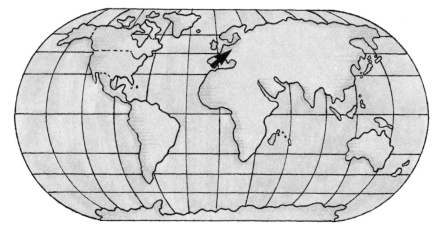

Greeting: *Joyeux Noël*, pronounced *joy-yooh no-el*, which means "Joyous Christmas." The greeting is in French.

How would you like to eat thirteen desserts on Christmas Eve? In southern France, you would. People serve a dessert to honor Jesus and one for each of his apostles. One of these desserts is a *bûche de Noël*, which means Yule log. It's a cake that represents a log that some French people burn in their homes from Christmas Day until New Year's Day for good luck. In certain parts of France, people cook their Christmas dinner over a Yule log.

Make some miniature Yule logs for your family and friends. Serve them during the Christmas season.

What you'll need:

- two ladyfingers or one Twinkie™ for each log
- chocolate frosting
- a knife to spread the frosting
- a fork
- powdered sugar
- holiday cake decorations such as holly, poinsettias, or colored sprinkles

What to do:

1. Spread frosting between the two ladyfingers. Stack them. Then spread frosting all over. Or, if you are using a Twinkie, spread frosting all over it.

2. Pull the fork over the frosting to make it look like bark.

3. Sprinkle with powdered sugar to resemble snow.

4. Add the decorations.

In parts of France, some children are visited by two gift bringers. Saint Nicholas comes from Spain on his white horse, the evening of December 5 or on December 6. He usually brings candy, fruit, coins, and nuts. On Christmas Eve, Père Noël arrives with more presents. He's similar to Santa Claus.

17

Germany

Greeting: *Fröhliche Weihnachten*, pronounced *freu-LISH-eh vi-NACH-ten*, which means "Merry Christmas." German is the official language of Germany.

Every day from December 1 through December 24, German children find a surprise hidden inside their Advent calendars. Advent calendars contain flaps or doors that mark these dates. Each day, children lift a flap or open a door to see what treat or picture lies beneath it. Some Advent calendars are so elaborate that they contain tiny drawers, boxes, or cloth bags.

Make an Advent calendar for yourself or for a friend.

What you'll need:

- a sheet of construction paper or tagboard 11 by 17 inches (28 by 43 cm)
- small stick-on notes
- a pen or fine-tipped marker
- holiday stickers
- candy or tiny toys
- tape
- crayons, colored markers, or glitter pens
- scissors

What to do:

1. Place the stick-on notes onto the construction paper or tagboard.

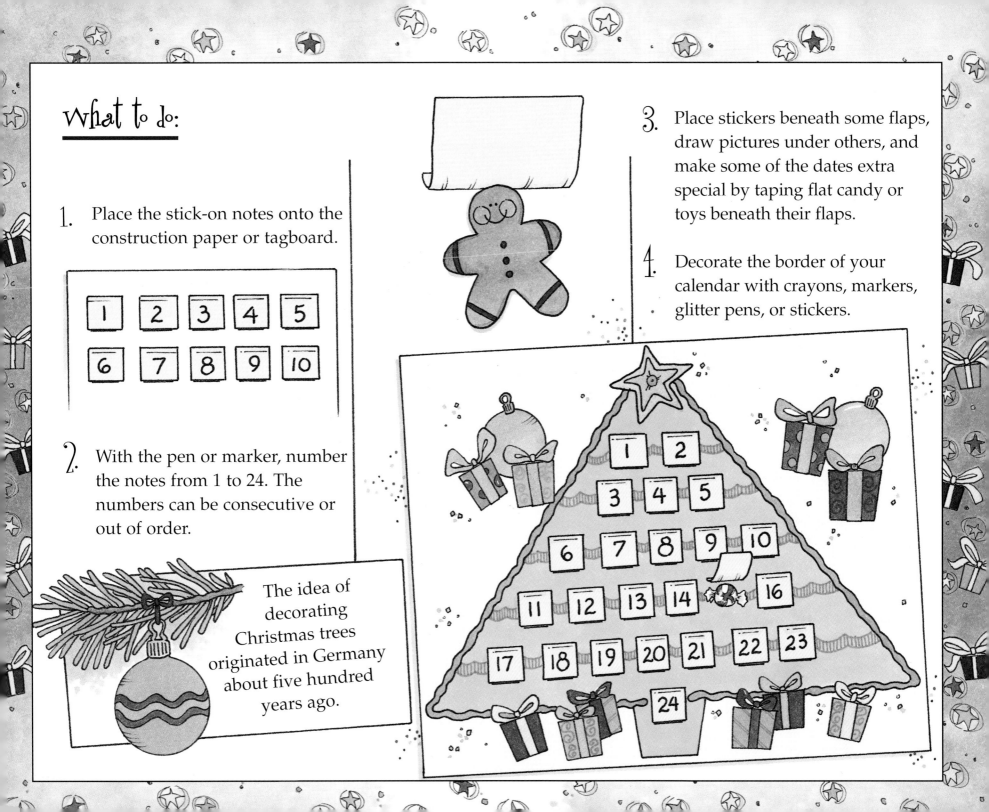

| 1 | 2 | 3 | 4 | 5 |
| 6 | 7 | 8 | 9 | 10 |

2. With the pen or marker, number the notes from 1 to 24. The numbers can be consecutive or out of order.

3. Place stickers beneath some flaps, draw pictures under others, and make some of the dates extra special by taping flat candy or toys beneath their flaps.

4. Decorate the border of your calendar with crayons, markers, glitter pens, or stickers.

The idea of decorating Christmas trees originated in Germany about five hundred years ago.

Ghana

Greeting: *Afishapa* pronounced *ah-fih-SHOP-uh*, which means "Merry Christmas and Happy New Year." Most people in Ghana speak English. Many people speak a tribal language, too. This greeting is in the tribal language called Akan.

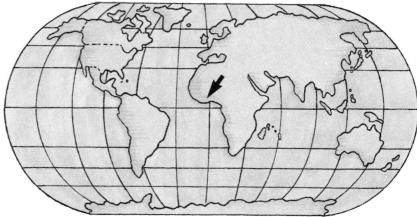

In Ghana, you might see Fire on the Mountain at Christmas time. Fire on the Mountain is a plant with yellowish-beige flowers. It blooms late in December in some parts of Ghana. You'll also see decorated guava, mango, and cashew trees in people's yards.

Inside, people display whispering pine trees festooned with crepe paper garlands that have designs cut into them. The decorations are handmade by Ghanaian children and their families. Sometimes people use cut-up old Christmas cards for decorations, too.

Make some crepe paper garlands and hang them on your Christmas tree.

What you'll need:

- a roll of crepe paper streamers
- scissors
- tape or a stapler to connect the strips

What to do:

1. Cut the crepe paper streamers into 3-foot (90-cm) pieces.

2. Fold each piece accordion-style.

3. Use your scissors to make cuts on the folds. Then unfold to see what kind of designs you've made.

4. Connect your strips with tape or staples. Make your garland long enough to place around your Christmas tree.

You can also use strips of tissue paper or colored paper to make your garlands.

21

Great Britain

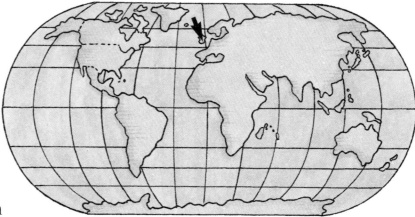

Greeting: *Happy Christmas* or *Merry Christmas*. The greeting is in English.

British people wear crowns while they eat Christmas dinner. They find them beside their dinner plates, inside a brightly colored tube called a Christmas cracker. When the cracker's ends are pulled, it makes a popping sound. Then people open it to find a toy, their fortune, a riddle, and the crown. Christmas dinner ends with flaming plum pudding for dessert. The pudding contains a lucky charm or coin for every child at the table.

   Make some crowns. Give them to your guests to wear during a Christmas dinner.

What you'll need:

- a tape measure
- scissors
- a strip of tissue paper measuring about 4 by 24 inches (10 by 60 cm)
- a stapler
- stickers (optional)

What to do:

1. Measure the heads of the people who will be wearing the crowns.

2. Cut the tissue paper to the proper length.

3. Staple the ends together.

4. Cut points.

In Great Britain, the crowns don't include stickers. You can add stickers to make your crowns more festive.

23

Greece

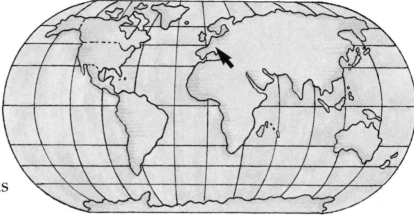

Greeting: *Kala Christouyena*, pronounced *kah-LAH chris-TOE-yen-uh*, which means "Merry Christmas." The greeting is in Greek.

Some Greek people believe that mischievous goblins visit their homes between Christmas and January 6. The ghosts might break dishes, turn out lights, or knock over chairs. They call the goblins *kalikántzari*. To keep the ghosts away, people sprinkle their homes with holy water.

On Christmas Day, Greek children go from house to house singing Christmas carols. They play drums, harmonicas, and triangles. Sometimes people give them candy, cookies, or coins.

You can make an instrument similar to a triangle. Here's how:

What you'll need:

- a wire clothes hanger
- scissors
- a tape measure
- yarn
- cellophane tape
- jingle bells

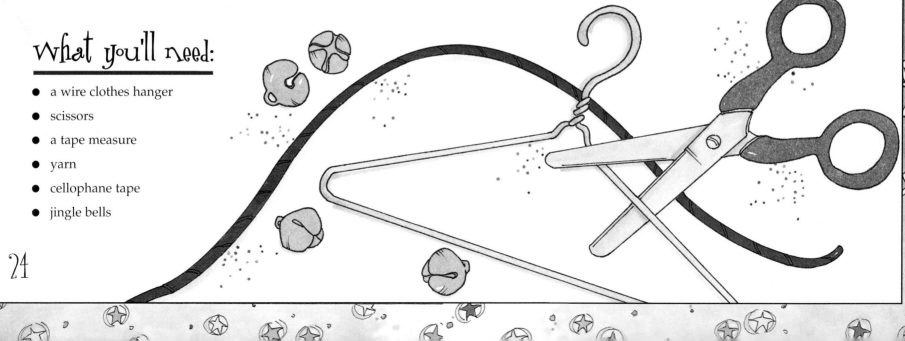

What to do:

1. Cover the end of the hanger handle with tape.

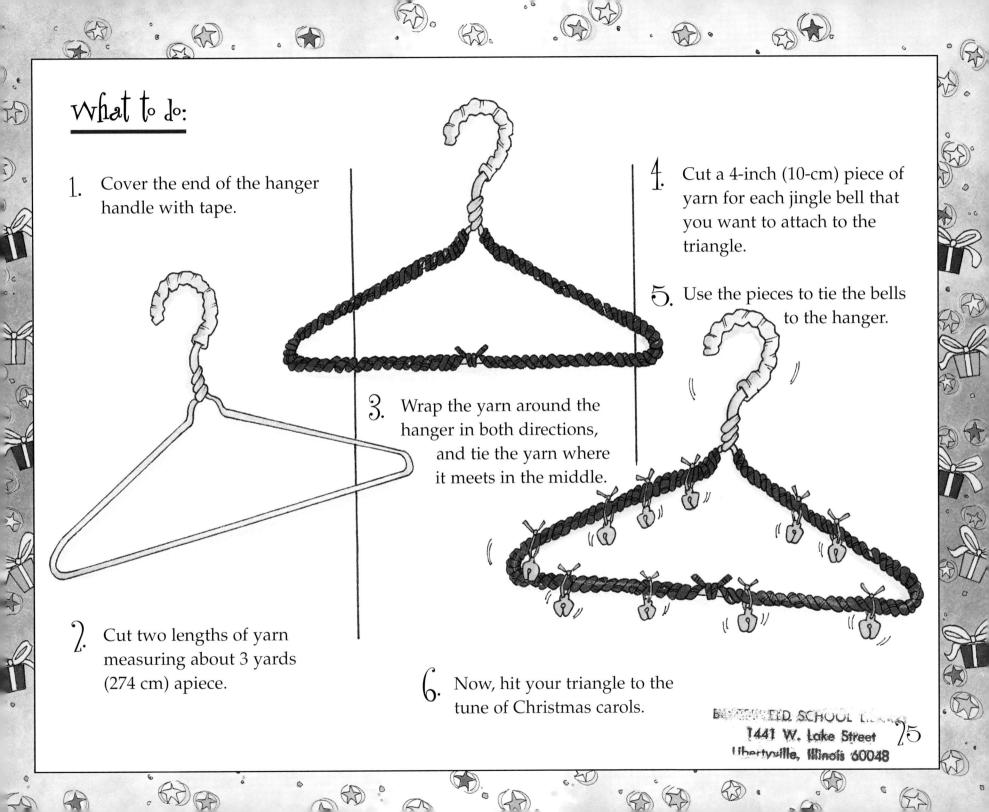

2. Cut two lengths of yarn measuring about 3 yards (274 cm) apiece.

3. Wrap the yarn around the hanger in both directions, and tie the yarn where it meets in the middle.

4. Cut a 4-inch (10-cm) piece of yarn for each jingle bell that you want to attach to the triangle.

5. Use the pieces to tie the bells to the hanger.

6. Now, hit your triangle to the tune of Christmas carols.

Iceland

Greeting: *Gledileg jól*, pronounced *gled-EH-leh yole*, which means "Merry Christmas." The greeting is in Icelandic.

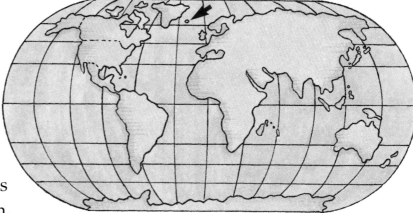

Some people believe that thirteen mischievous elves visit Icelandic children during the Christmas season. The first elf arrives on December 12. The last one comes on December 24. They leave gifts in the children's shoes. Then the elves gradually go back to the mountains, one by one. By January 6, the elves are gone and the Christmas season is over.

Icelandic children decorate their homes with Christmas pockets and mouse stairs. Christmas pockets are woven hearts. Mouse stairs are woven chains of colored construction paper. Make some Christmas pockets and hang them on your Christmas tree or around your house.

What you'll need:

- a pencil
- a ruler
- two 5-inch (13-cm) squares of construction paper (each sheet should be a different color)
- scissors
- yarn

What to do:

1. Hand-copy, trace, or photocopy the hump pattern. You will need two humps for each heart.

2. Cut out the humps.

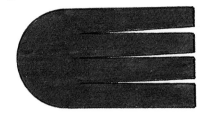

3. Cut on the dark lines to make slits.

4. Weave the slits together to form a heart.

5. Attach the yarn to your heart and hang it on your Christmas tree.

The thirteen elves have different names that describe their mischief. Here are some of the most common names used. Draw pictures of some of the elves. Think of some new names to describe them.

Window Peeper	Yogurt Gobbler
Donut Beggar	Fat Gobbler
Ice Breaker	Skirt Blower
Sausage Snatcher	Doorway Sniffer
Pot Licker	Smoke Gulper
Door Slammer	Itty Bitty
Butter Greedy	

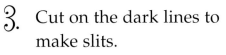

On December 13, the oldest girl in the house dresses in a long white gown with a red sash. She places a crown of candles decorated with evergreen boughs on her head. Then she serves buns and coffee to her family. St. Lucia Day is celebrated in Sweden, Finland, Norway, and Denmark, too. It honors Saint Lucia, the patron saint of light.

India

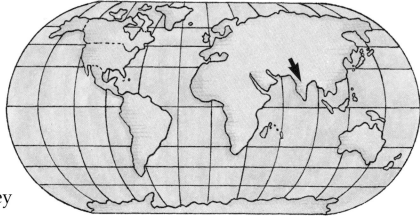

Greeting: Merry Christmas

The greeting is in English, which is one of the sixteen languages spoken in India.

In some parts of India, people celebrate Christmas by setting up a banana tree in their house. Then they decorate it with lots of glittering ornaments. People cover their ceilings from corner to corner with streamers, fancy garlands, and balloons. Outside their homes, they light candles and display a star near their front door. The star reminds people of how the Three Kings found their way to Bethlehem.

Hang some glittery garlands from your ceiling or Christmas tree. Here's how to make them:

What you'll need:

- a ruler or tape measure
- cash register tape
- scissors
- glue
- stapler and staples to connect the strips of cash register tape, if you want to make a garland that measures longer than 3 feet (90 cm)
- things to decorate your garland: crayons, markers, glitter pens, ribbon, star stickers, sequins or tinsel, strips cut from a star garland (you can purchase star garlands at a craft or party store)

28

What to do:

1. Cut the cash register tape into 3-foot (90-cm) lengths. This length will be manageable to work with. You can make the garland as long as you want by stapling the tapes together.

2. Decorate the cash register tape with crayons, markers, and glitter pens. Attach stickers and sequins with glue.

3. Glue tinsel, strips of ribbon, and star garland strips to the edges of the cash register tape.

Note: This craft can be a group project. At home, family members may each work on a different section of a long garland. At school, class members can each contribute a section to a long garland to decorate the classroom.

Jamaica

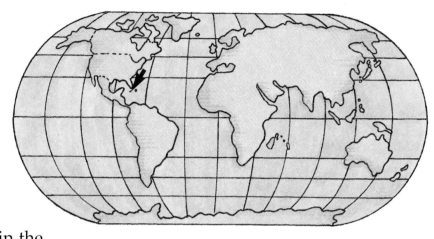

Greeting: Merry Christmas. The official language of Jamaica is English.

Jamaican people welcome Christmas with a celebration called *Jonkonnu*, which can occur on December 24, 25, or 26. During *Jonkonnu*, people watch parades or participate in them. They dance in the street. People dress up as animals, kings, queens, princesses, or a character known as the Pitchy Patchy man. His costume contains hundreds of different-colored strips of fabrics. People play drums, blow whistles, play bamboo flutes, and shake tassels to the music.

Make a tassel to shake to the tune of Caribbean music on December 26.

What you'll need:

- a tape measure or ruler
- scissors
- twelve pieces of yarn or ribbon about 12 inches (30 cm) long

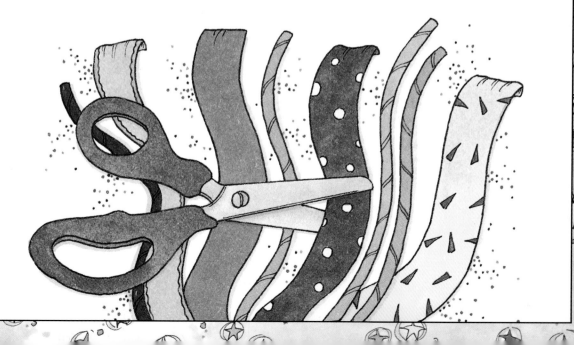

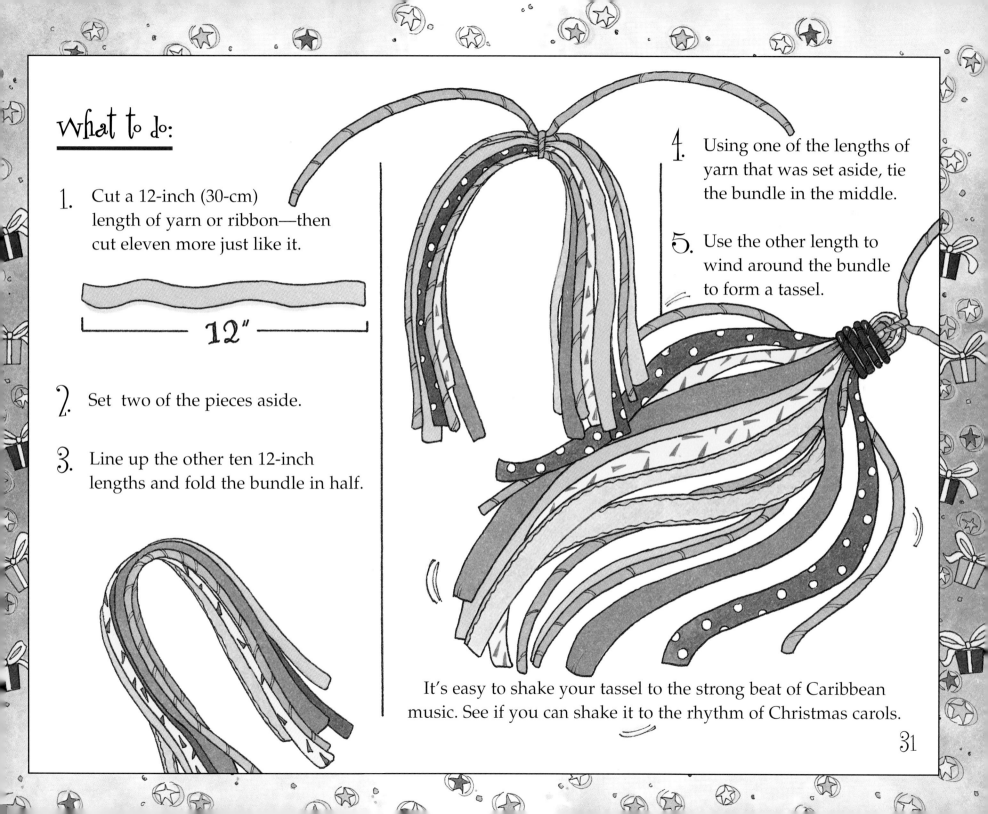

What to do:

1. Cut a 12-inch (30-cm) length of yarn or ribbon—then cut eleven more just like it.

12"

2. Set two of the pieces aside.

3. Line up the other ten 12-inch lengths and fold the bundle in half.

4. Using one of the lengths of yarn that was set aside, tie the bundle in the middle.

5. Use the other length to wind around the bundle to form a tassel.

It's easy to shake your tassel to the strong beat of Caribbean music. See if you can shake it to the rhythm of Christmas carols.

31

Japan

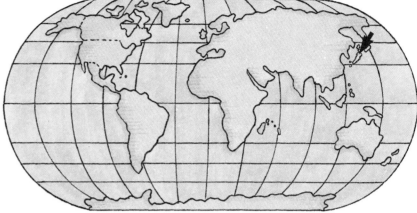

Greeting: *Meri Kurisumasu*, pronounced *meh-REE kur-i-sue-MAH-sue*, which means "Merry Christmas." The greeting is in Japanese.

You can be sure that the Christmas season has arrived in Japan when you see Christmas cakes in almost every bakery. A Christmas cake is a round cake decorated with white frosting, strawberries, and holiday ornaments. Japanese people serve their cakes on Christmas Eve. In the morning, children hope to find gifts from Santa Kurohsu (pronounced *koo-ROW-sue*) or Hoteiosho (pronounced *hoe-TAY-oh-sue*), a priest with eyes in the back of his head. Either one might leave presents beneath an evergreen tree decorated with tiny candles, dolls, wind chimes, and gold paper fans.

Make some gold fans and hang them from your Christmas tree.

What you'll need:

- a sheet of gold wrapping paper about 8½ by 11 inches (22 by 28 cm) (enough for two fans)
- scissors
- a ruler
- a stapler
- a pencil
- red yarn or ribbon about 10 inches (25 cm) long

What to do:

1. Cut the paper in half lengthwise.

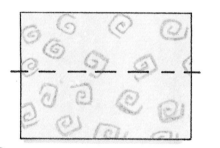

2. Fold each sheet accordion style lengthwise.

3. Fold in half so the ends meet.

4. Staple ½ inch (1 cm) up from the bottom of the fan.

5. Use the pencil to form an opening above the staple.

6. Insert the ribbon or yarn through the opening and tie the ends together to form a loop.

7. Hang the fan from your Christmas tree.

Children go to school on Christmas day in Japan. Christmas is not a national holiday in Japan, because few people follow the Christian religion. But many Japanese people have adopted the custom of decorating Christmas trees and giving gifts.

Lebanon

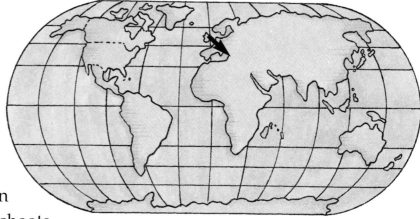

Greeting: *Meelad Majeed*, pronounced *mee-LAHD mah-JEED*, which means "Birth Glorious." The greeting is in Arabic.

About a month before Christmas, Lebanese children plant wheat grains, lentils, or bean seeds in small dishes. As Christmas nears, the seeds sprout shoots from 3 to 6 inches (8 to 15 cm) high. Children use the shoots to decorate their family's home and the manger scene, which is usually beneath the Christmas tree. The manger scene does not include Baby Jesus until December 24. Lebanese families place him in the manger at midnight on Christmas Eve. That's when bells ring throughout Lebanon to announce the anniversary of Christ's birth.

Grow some shoots from seeds. Place them by a nativity scene beneath your Christmas tree.

What you'll need:

- a small dish
- cotton balls (these seeds don't need to grow in dirt)
- wheat grains, lentils, or bean seeds
- water

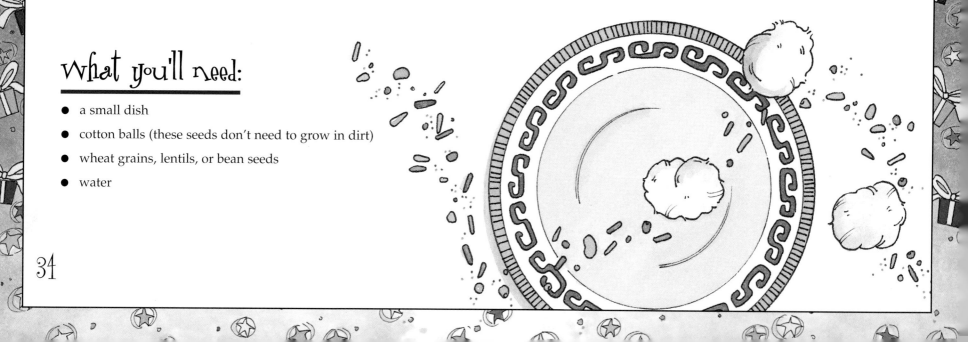

What to do:

1. Put the cotton balls into the dish.

2. Put your seeds on the cotton.

3. Sprinkle water on the cotton.

4. Water the cotton daily to keep it damp.

In Lebanon at Christmastime people serve a special soup called *sheesh barak*. The soup is so difficult to make that people eat it only once a year.

Mexico

Greeting: *Feliz Navidad*, pronounced *feh-LEES nah-VEE-dad*, which means "Happy Nativity." The official language of Mexico is Spanish.

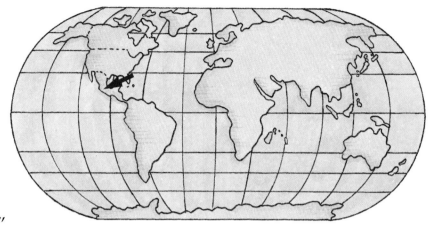

Mexican children begin their Christmas celebrations nine days before Christmas with the festival of *Posadas*. *Posada* means "shelter" or "inn." Each evening, groups of people enact the journey of Mary and Joseph. They knock on neighbors' doors until they find a family that lets them inside and pretends to be innkeepers. Then they have a party.

    On Christmas Eve they receive a visit from Santa Claus, who brings gifts. On the evening of January 5, the Three Kings arrive on their camels with more presents. Children put their shoes or boxes filled with hay by their beds so the camels can have a snack. Some children also leave dishes of water.

    Make a box for the Three Kings, too. Put it by your bed on the evening of January 5. Maybe the Kings will come with gifts.

What you'll need:

- an empty shoe box
- a paintbrush
- poster paint
- star stickers and/or any type of holiday stickers
- hay (you can buy it at a pet store or make your own by shredding yellow construction or tissue paper)

What to do:

1. Paint the outside of your shoe box.

2. When the paint dries, decorate the box with stickers.

3. Place the hay in the box.

Before Three Kings' Day, children send notes to the Kings, telling them how good they've been and letting them know what they want. Write letters to them in your best writing. Their names are Gaspar, Melchior, and Baltazar in Spanish.

Nigeria

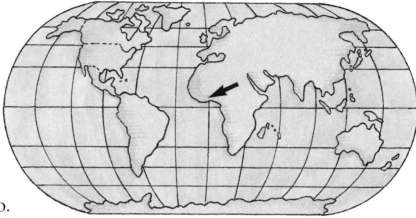

Greeting: *Eku Odun Ebi Jesu*, pronounced *EH-koo oh-DONE eh-BEE hay-SUE*, which means "Happy Celebration on the birth of Jesus Christ." The greeting is in Yoruba, the language of the Yoruba people. The major language of Nigeria is English, but many people use a tribal language, too.

Nigerian people might light sparklers and dress in costume at Christmastime. Then they walk from house to house and act out the Christmas story for their neighbors. Often they receive money, which they donate to their church.

Nigerians decorate palm trees at Christmas instead of evergreen trees. They hang palm branches inside and outside their homes. Nigerians consider palm branches a sign of peace and a symbol of Christmas.

Make a palm leaf to display in your home during the Christmas season.

What you'll need:

- 8½- by 11-inch sheet (20- by 28-cm) of green construction paper
- a pencil
- scissors
- a ruler
- a strip of brown construction paper measuring about 1 inch (2.5 cm) wide
- glue
- glitter

38

What to do:

1. Fold your green construction paper in half lengthwise. Draw a pattern of a half leaf with a pencil.

2. Cut around the pattern. Make sure not to cut on the fold.

3. Cut the edges to make fringes.

4. Unfold.

5. Glue the strip of brown paper along the center to make a stem, so that a few inches (about 8 cm) stick out from the bottom of the leaf.

6. Decorate the palm leaf with gold glitter.

The Philippines

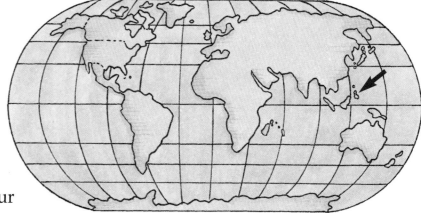

Greeting: *Maligayang Pasko*, pronounced *mali-gay-ANG pahs-CO*, which means "Merry Christmas." The greeting is in Tagalog, one of the languages spoken in the Philippines.

The Christmas season begins on December 16 at four o'clock in the morning with bells. They ring all over the Philippines, announcing the first mass of the Christmas season. This is the time of year that Filipino people exhibit three-dimensional paper stars called *parols*. People display *parols* small enough to hang on a Christmas tree or stars that measure 30 feet (9 meters) wide. Some people buy their *parols*. Others spend months making them. Towns hold parades of stars on Christmas Eve and give prizes for the best *parols*.

You can make a *parol* out of craft sticks and paper. Here's how:

What you'll need:

- a ruler
- scissors
- two triangles of construction paper measuring 4 inches (10 cm) on each side. You can have an adult premeasure and cut these for you, or you can measure and cut them yourself.
- glue
- two craft sticks
- star stickers
- six pieces of curly paper ribbon measuring about 4 inches (10 cm) long

40

What to do:

1. Cut two triangles from construction paper, measuring 4 inches (10 cm) on each side.

2. Place your triangles so that they form a star.

3. Glue the triangles together.

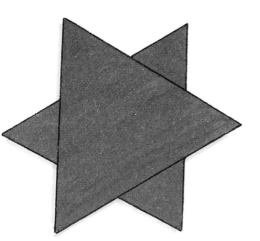

4. Glue the craft sticks together so that they form an X.

5. Glue the craft-stick X to the center of the star so that the ends stick out between the points of the star.

6. Decorate the *parol* with star stickers. You can decorate the craft sticks, too.

7. Glue the paper ribbon pieces to the tips of the *parol*'s points.

Poland

Greeting: *Wesołych Świąt*, pronounced *veh-SO-wig shi-vi-ANT*, which means Merry Christmas. The greeting is in Polish.

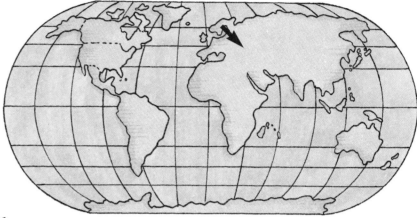

You might find spiders or a spider's web on a Polish Christmas tree. A legend says that a spider wove a blanket for Baby Jesus. So Polish people consider spiders to be symbols of prosperity and good luck at Christmas. Polish people also decorate their trees with candy, fruit, nuts, and homemade decorations made from eggs.

On Christmas Eve, Polish families set an extra place at their table in case an unexpected guest arrives. They place straw on their table, too. The straw reminds them of the stable where Jesus was born.

What you'll need:

- one sheet of 8½- by 11-inch (22- by 26-cm) black construction paper
- scissors
- glue
- wiggle eyes
- ribbon, a small stick-on bow, or a foil snowflake to decorate the spider
- a pencil
- yarn

What to do:

1. Fold the paper in half horizontally.

2. Cut into two separate sheets. One sheet will be for making the spider's head and body. The other sheet will be for constructing the spider's legs.

3. From one sheet, cut a large circle for the spider's body and a smaller circle for the head.

4. Cut 8 strips from the other sheet, using about half of it. The strips will become the spider's legs.

5. Glue the head to the body

6. Fold the strips accordion style. Glue the legs to the spider's body.

7. Now add the wiggle eyes to the spider's head.

8. Decorate the spider's body with the ribbon, bow, or snowflake.

Some Polish people have two Christmas trees in their home—a big one and a small one. The small one hangs upside down in the kitchen. The small tree symbolizes a tree that people long ago hung inside their barns at Christmas. They put food for their animals on it.

9. Poke a tiny hole in the spider's back with the pencil. Put the yarn through the hole and tie it to make a loop.

43

Hang the spider on your Christmas tree.

Puerto Rico

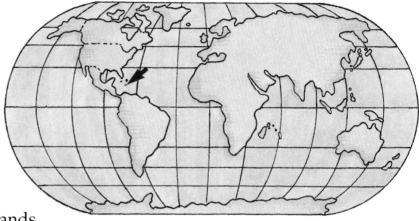

Greeting: *Feliz Navidad,* pronounced *feh-LEES nah-VEE-dad,* which means "Happy Nativity." The greeting is in Spanish.

At Christmastime in Puerto Rico, you might wake up at any time of night to the sounds of a band playing lively Christmas carols. People call these bands *parrandas. Parranda* players gather with maracas, drums, and guitars. They may use pots and pans, too. They surprise their friends by stopping in front of their homes to perform. The musicians are often invited inside and given food. Sometimes their hosts join the group, so the *parranda* band grows. The music may not end until three o'clock in the morning.

Make a maraca. Have your friends make some, too. Shake them to the rhythm of Christmas carols or a CD of Salsa music.

What you'll need:

- an empty 8- to 12-ounce (237- to 355-milliliter) plastic bottle with screw-on top, shaped so that the end can be used as a handle
- dried beans or rice
- poster paint
- a paintbrush
- stickers
- glue
- crepe paper or tissue paper to cover the neck of the bottle

44

What to do:

1. Put beans or rice into the bottle.

2. Screw the cap onto the bottle tightly.

3. Paint the bottle.

4. When your bottle is dry, add stickers to decorate it.

5. Glue the crepe paper or tissue paper to the neck and cap of the bottle to cover them.

6. Now, shake your maraca to the tunes of Christmas carols.

Christmas lasts through Three Kings' Day in Puerto Rico. Then Puerto Rican people have eight more days of celebrations called Octavitas, which means "little eights."

45

Serbia

Greeting: *Sretan Božič*, pronounced *SRE-tahn BOE-zick*, which means "Merry Christmas." The greeting is in Serbian.

At dawn on Christmas, Serbian people toss wheat seeds and nuts at a visitor called a *Polaznik*. The *Polaznik* is a male who is special to the family, and the first person to enter the house on Christmas. In Serbia, people celebrate Christmas on January 7, according to the Julian calendar.

The *Polaznik* sits at the head of the table during Christmas meals. He's the first guest to taste the roast pig that is served at the family's Christmas dinner along with a bread called *cesnica* (pronounced *chez-NEETZ-zuh*). *Cesnica* is a round loaf of bread with a silver coin baked inside. Everyone touches the bread before it's cut and served. The person who receives the slice containing the coin will have good luck until next Christmas.

Make *cesnica*. Serve it at Christmas to see who gets good luck.

What you'll need:

- two tubes of refrigerated hot roll mix
- a round cake pan
- a silver coin
- a piece of wax paper for wrapping the silver coin

46

What to do:

1. Put the rolls into the cake pan. Smooth the tops so they connect. You may have a few leftover rolls. Bake them separately.

2. Wash the coin. Place it in wax paper. Hide it in the dough.

3. Bake the rolls according to package directions. You may need to bake a few minutes longer for the *cesnica* to be nicely browned.

4. Cool the *cesnica*. Make sure everyone has a chance to touch it before it's cut and served.

47

Bibliography

Christmas Greetings Page:
   http://members.aol.com/wscaswell/message.htm

Christmas in Canada. Chicago: World Book, 1994.

Christmas in Germany. Lincolnwood, IL: Passport Books, 1995.

Beardon, Hannah. *Bolivia.* Danbury, CT: Grolier Educational, 1999.

Chambers, Catherine. *A World of Holidays: Christmas.* Austin, TX: Raintree Steck-Vaughn Publishers, 1997.

Cooke, Tim. *Jamaica.* Danbury, CT: Grolier Educational, 1997.

Dawson, Susie. *Mexico.* Danbury, CT: Grolier Educational, 1997.

Dvergsten Stevens, Beth. *Celebrate Christmas Around the World.* Huntington Beach, CA: Teacher Created Materials, 1994.

Fowler, Virginia. *Christmas Crafts and Customs Around the World.* Englewood Cliffs, NJ: Prentice-Hall, 1984.

Goldsmith, Terrence. *Christmas Around the World: A Celebration.* Dorset, England: New Orchard Editions, 1985.

Griffiths, Diana. *Australia.* Milwaukee: Gareth Stevens Publishing, 1999.

Herda, D.J. *Christmas.* New York: Franklin Watts, 1983.

Hoyt-Goldsmith, Diane. *Las Posadas: An Hispanic Christmas Celebration.* New York: Holiday House, 1999.

Hughes, Ellen. *Christmas in Australia.* Chicago: World Book, 1998.

Illsley, Linda. *The Caribbean.* Austin, TX: Raintree Steck-Vaughn Publishers, 1999.

Jones, Lynda. *Kids Around the World Celebrate!* New York: John Wiley & Sons, 2000.

Kelley, Emily. *Christmas Around the World.* Minneapolis: Carolrhoda Books, 1986.

Kennedy, Pamela. *A Christmas Celebration.* Nashville, TN: Ideals Publishing, 1992.

Lankford, Mary D. *Christmas Around the World.* New York: Morrow Junior Books, 1995.

Lord, Richard. *Germany.* Milwaukee: Gareth Stevens Publishing, 1997.

Madden Ross, Corrine. *Christmas in France.* Chicago: World Book, 1988.

McKay, Susan. *France.* Milwaukee: Gareth Stevens Publishing, 1998.

Paul, Tessa. *England.* Danbury, CT: Grolier Educational, 1999.

Phillips, Charles. *France.* Danbury, CT: Grolier Educational, 1999.

Rodriguez, Dr. Aurea. *Puerto Rico.* Danbury, CT: Grolier Educational, 1999.

Ross, Corrine. *Christmas in Italy.* Chicago: World Book, 1988.

Sechrist, Elizabeth Hough. *Christmas Everywhere.* Philadelphia: Macrae Smith, 1936.

Thompson, Paul. *Poland.* Danbury, CT: Grolier Educational, 1999.

Wernecke, Herbert H. *Christmas Customs Around the World.* Philadelphia: Westminster Press, 1959.

Winchester, Faith. H*ispanic Holidays.* Mankato, MN: Bridgestone Books, 1996.

Zwierzynska-Coldicott, Aldona Maria. *Poland.* Milwaukee: Gareth Stevens Publishing, 1998.